LEADER'S GUIDE

SHIFTING ATMOSPHERES

Other Book by Dawna De Silva

SOZO (with Teresa Liebscher)

LEADER'S GUIDE

SHIFTING ATMOSPHERES

DISCERNING & DISPLACING
THE SPIRITUAL FORCES
AROUND YOU

DAWNA DE SILVA

DESTINY IMAGE® PUBLISHERS, INC.
P.O. Box 310, Shippensburg, PA 17257-0310
"Promoting Inspired Lives."

This book and all other Destiny Image and Destiny Image Fiction books are available at Christian bookstores and distributors worldwide.

Interior design by Terry Clifton

For more information on foreign distributors, call 717-532-3040.
Reach us on the Internet: www.destinyimage.com.

ISBN 13 TP: 978-0-7684-1570-4

For Worldwide Distribution, Printed in the U.S.A.
1 2 3 4 5 6 7 8 / 21 20 19 18 17

Contents

Basic Leader Guidelines

Here are some of the ways you can use the curriculum:

1. Church Small Group

Often, churches feature a variety of different small group opportunities per season in terms of books, curriculum resources, and Bible studies. *Shifting Atmospheres* would be included among the offering of titles for whatever season you are launching for the small group program.

It is recommended that you have at least four to five people to make up a small group and a maximum of twelve. If you end up with more than twelve members, either the group needs to multiply and break into two different groups or you should consider moving toward a church class model (which will be outlined below).

For a small group setting, here are the essentials:

- *Meeting place*: Either the leader's home or a space provided by the church.
- *Appropriate technology*: A DVD player attached to a TV that is large enough for all of the group members to see (and loud enough for everyone to hear).
- *Leader/Facilitator*: This person will often be the host, if the small group is being conducted at someone's home; but it can also be a team (husband/wife, two church leaders, etc.). The leader(s) will direct the session from beginning to end, from sending reminder e-mails to participating group members about the

meetings, to closing out the sessions in prayer and dismissing everyone. That said, leaders might select certain people in the group to assist with various elements of the meeting— worship, prayer, ministry time, etc. A detailed description of what the group meetings should look like will follow in the pages to come.

Sample Schedule for Home Group Meeting (for a 7:00 P.M. Meeting)

- Before arrival: Ensure that refreshments are ready by 6:15 P.M. If they need to be refrigerated, ensure they are preserved appropriately until 15 minutes prior to the official meeting time.

- 6:15 P.M.: Leaders arrive at meeting home or facility.

- 6:15–6:25 P.M.: Connect with hosts, co-hosts, and/or co-leaders to review the evening's program.

- 6:25–6:35 P.M.: Pray with hosts, co-hosts, and/or co-leaders for the evening's events. Here are some sample prayer directives:
  - For the Holy Spirit to move and minister freely.
  - For the teaching to connect with and transform all who hear it.
  - For dialogue and conversation that edifies.
  - For comfort and transparency among group members.
  - For the presence of God to manifest during worship.
  - For testimonies of answered prayers.
  - For increased hunger for God's presence and power.

- 6:35–6:45 P.M.: Ensure technology is functioning properly.

Test the DVD featuring the teaching session, making sure it is set up to the appropriate session.

If you are doing praise and worship without a live worship leader, ensure that either the music player is functional, set at an appropriate volume (not soft, but not incredibly loud), and that song sheets are available for everyone so they can sing along with the lyrics. (If you are tech savvy, you could do a PowerPoint or Keynote presentation featuring the lyrics.)

- 6:45–7:00 P.M.: Welcome and greet people as they come.

- 7:00–7:10 P.M.: Enjoy connecting over refreshments.

- 7:10–7:12 P.M.: Gather everyone together in the meeting place.
- 7:12–7:30 P.M.: Pray to open up worship. Worship together.
- 7:30–7:40 P.M.: Have ministry and prayer time or open it up for discussion for people to share what they have noticed has changed spiritually around them or in them since the last *Shifting Atmospheres* session.
- 7:40–8:00 P.M.: Watch DVD session.
- 8:00–8:20 P.M.: Discuss DVD session.
- 8:20–8:35 P.M.: Do the group activation.
- 8:35–8:40 P.M.: Close in prayer and dismiss.

This sample schedule is *not* intended to lock you into a formula. It is simply provided as a template to help you get started. Our hope is that you customize it according to the unique needs of your group and sensitively navigate the activity of the Holy Spirit as He uses these sessions to supernaturally transform the lives of every person participating in the study.

2. Small Group Church-Wide Campaign

This would be the decision of the pastor or senior leadership of the church. In this model, the entire church would go through *Shifting Atmospheres* in both the main services and ancillary small groups/life classes.

These campaigns would be marketed as *40 Days of Shifting the Atmosphere* or *40 Days to Shift the Atmospheres Around You*. The pastor's weekend sermon would be based on the principles in *Shifting Atmospheres,* and the Sunday school classes/life classes and/or small groups would also follow the *Shifting Atmospheres* curriculum format.

3. Church Class | Mid-Week Class | Sunday School Curriculum

Churches of all sizes offer a variety of classes purposed to develop members into more effective disciples of Jesus and agents of transformation in their spheres of influence. *Shifting Atmospheres* brings practical tools to both overcome negative strongholds as individuals and rise up to take our place of authority by bringing Heaven to earth.

Typically, churches offer a variety of topical classes targeted at men's needs, women's needs, marriage, family, finances, and various areas of Bible study. *Shifting Atmospheres* is a unique resource, as it does not fit in with the aforementioned traditional topics usually offered to the Church body. On the contrary, this study breaks down what it means to influence the spiritual atmosphere around us, and shows believers how to supernaturally transform the world around them. As atmospheres are shifted from negative to positive, people are able to think and act like who God intends them to be.

While it may difficult to facilitate dialogue in a class setting, it is certainly optional and recommended. The other way to successfully engage *Shifting Atmospheres* in a class setting is to have a teacher/leader go through the questions/answers presented in the upcoming pages and use these as his or her teaching notes.

4. Individual Study

While the curriculum is designed for use in a group setting, it also works as a tool that can equip anyone who is looking to gain more freedom personally and bring corporate freedom in the spirit realm.

STEPS TO LAUNCHING A *SHIFTING ATMOSPHERES* GROUP OR CLASS

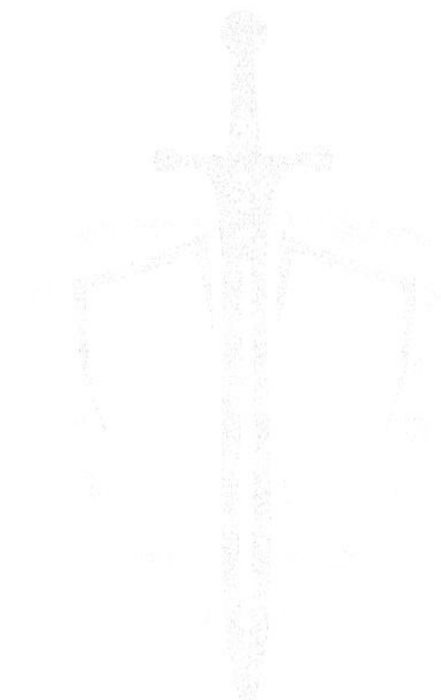

PREPARE WITH PRAYER!

Pray! If you are a **church leader**, prayerfully consider how *Shifting Atmospheres* could transform the culture and climate of your church community! The Lord is raising up bodies of believers who bring transformation in their wake because of the overflow of a mind that's been reoriented to Heaven's perspective. Spend some time with the Holy Spirit, asking Him to give you vision for what this unique study will do for your church, and, ultimately, how a Kingdom-minded people will transform your city and region.

If you are a **group leader** or **class facilitator**, pray for those who will be attending your group, signing up for your class, and will be positioning their lives to be transformed by the power and presence of God in this study.

PREPARE PRACTICALLY!

Determine how you will be using the Shifting Atmospheres curriculum.

Identify which of the following formats you will be using the curriculum in:

- Church-sponsored small group study
- Church-wide campaign
- Church class (Wednesday night, Sunday morning, etc.)
- Individual study

Determine a meeting location and ensure availability of appropriate equipment.

Keep in mind the number of people who may attend. You will also need AV (audio-visual) equipment. The more comfortable the setting, the more people will enjoy being there, and will spend more time ministering to each other! A word of caution here: the larger the group, the greater the need for co-leaders or assistants. The ideal small group size is difficult to judge; however, once you get more than ten to twelve people, it becomes difficult for each member to feel "heard." If your group is larger than twelve people, consider either having two or more small group discussion leaders or "multiplying" the larger group into two smaller ones.

Determine the format for your meetings.

The presence of the Lord, which brings transformation, is cradled and stewarded well in the midst of organization. Structure should never replace spontaneity; on the contrary, having a plan and determining what type of format your meetings will take enables you to flow with the Holy Spirit and minister more effectively.

Also, by determining what kind of meeting you will be hosting, you become well equipped to develop a schedule for the meeting, identify potential co-leaders, and order the appropriate number of resources.

Set a schedule for your meetings.

Once you have established the format for your meetings, set a schedule for your meetings. Some groups like to have a time of fellowship or socializing (either before or after the meeting begins) where light refreshments are offered. Some groups will want to incorporate times of worship and personal ministry into the small group or class. This is highly recommended for *Shifting Atmospheres*, as the study is designed to equip and activate believers through being in tune with what Father God, Jesus, and Holy Spirit are saying. The video portion and discussion questions are intended to instruct believers, while the worship, times of ministry, group interaction, prayer time, and activation elements are purposed to engage them to live out what they just learned. *Shifting Atmospheres* is not an airy-fairy concept; it is a practical reality for every born-again believer. This study is intended to educate; but even more so, it is designed to activate believers and position them to steward their personal as well as corporate atmospheres.

Establish a start date along with a weekly meeting day and time.

This eight-week curriculum should be followed consistently and consecutively. Be mindful of the fact that while there are eight weeks of material, most groups will want to meet one last time after completing the last week to celebrate, or designate their first meeting as a time to get to know each other and "break the ice." This is very normal and should be encouraged to continue the community momentum that the small group experience initiates. Typically, after the final session is completed, groups will often engage in a social activity—either having a barbeque or going out to dinner together, having a game night, or something of the like.

Look far enough ahead on the calendar to account for anything that might interfere. Choose a day that works well for the members of your group. For a church class, be sure to coordinate the time with the appropriate ministry leader.

Advertise!

Getting the word out in multiple ways is most effective. Print out flyers, post a sign-up sheet, make an announcement in church services or group meetings, send out weekly e-mails and text messages, set up your own blog or website, or post the event on the social media avenue you and your group utilize most (Facebook, Twitter, etc.). A personal invitation or phone call is a great way to reach those who might need that little bit of extra encouragement to get involved.

For any type of small group or class to succeed, it must be endorsed by and encouraged from the leadership. For larger churches with multiple group/class offerings, it is wise to provide church members literature featuring all of the different small group/class options. This information should also be displayed online in an easily accessible page on your church website.

For smaller churches, it is a good idea for the pastor or a key leader to announce the launch of a small group course or class from the pulpit during an announcement time.

Gather your materials.

Each leader will need the *Shifting Atmospheres* Leader's Kit. Additionally, each participant will need a personal copy of the *Shifting Atmospheres* study guide and book.

We have found it best for the materials to all be purchased at one time—many booksellers and distributors offer discounts on multiple orders, and you are assured that each member will have their materials from the beginning of the course.

Step Forward!

Arrive at your meeting in *plenty* of time to prepare; frazzled last-minute preparations do not put you in a place of "rest," and your group members will sense your stress. Ensure that all AV equipment is working properly and that you have ample supplies for each member. Name tags are a great idea, at least for the first couple of meetings. Icebreaker and introduction activities are also a good idea for the first meeting.

Pray for your members. As much as possible, make yourself available to them. As members increase in discerning and shifting the spirit realm, they will want to share that discovery! You will also need to encourage those who struggle, grow weary, or lose heart along the journey. Make sure your members stay committed so they experience the full benefits of this teaching.

Embrace the journey that you and your fellow members are embarking on. Make sure you are going through the study guide along with your group members, doing the exercises, and trying out the new things you're learning about. Transformation begins within *you*!

Multiply yourself. Is there someone you know who was not able to attend your group, heard about it partway through, or had an interest in going through it after you finished? Help them to initiate their own small group by giving them tips now that you know how to host *Shifting Atmospheres* in a group setting!

Thank You

Thank you for embarking on a journey to equip the bride of Christ to be powerful, peaceful, joyful, and who she is destined to be in this world.

Leader Checklist

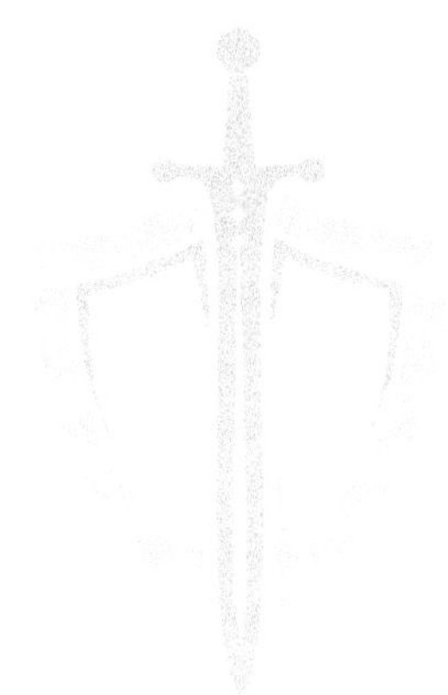

One to Two Months Prior

______ Have you determined a start date for your class or small group?

______ Have you determined the format, meeting day and time, and weekly meeting schedule?

______ Have you selected a meeting location (making sure you have adequate space and AV equipment available)?

______ Have you advertised? Do you have a sign-up sheet to ensure you order enough materials?

Three Weeks to One Month Prior

______ Have you ordered materials? You will need a copy of *Shifting Atmospheres* Leader's Kit, along with copies of the workbook and book for each participant.

______ Have you organized your meeting schedule/format?

One to Two Weeks Prior

______ Have you received all your materials?

______ Have you reviewed the DVDs and your Leader's Kit to familiarize yourself with the material and to ensure everything is in order?

______ Have you planned and organized the refreshments, if you are planning to provide them? Some leaders will handle this themselves, and some find it easier to allow participants to sign up to provide refreshments if they would like to do so.

______ Have you advertised and promoted? This includes sending out e-mail to all participants, setting up a Facebook group, setting up a group through your church's database system (if available), promotion in the church bulletin, etc.

______ Have you appointed co-leaders to assist you with the various portions of the group/class? While it is not necessary, it is helpful to have someone who is in charge of either leading (on guitar, keyboard, etc.) or arranging the worship music (choosing songs and creating song lyric sheets, etc.). It is also helpful to have a prayer coordinator as well—someone who helps facilitate the prayer time, ensuring that all of the prayer needs are acknowledged and remembered, and assigning the various requests to group members who are willing to lift up those needs in prayer.

First Meeting Day

______ Plan to arrive *early!* Give yourself extra time to set up the meeting space, double check all AV equipment, and organize your materials. It might be helpful to ask participants to arrive 15 minutes early for the first meeting to allow for greeting and introducing everyone to each other, giving out name tags, distributing materials, and doing any icebreaker activities you might have planned.

Discussion Questions

Weekly Overview of Meetings/ Group Sessions

Here are some instructions on how to use each of the weekly Discussion Question guides.

Welcome and Fellowship Time
(10–15 minutes)

This usually begins five to ten minutes prior to the designated meeting time and typically continues up until ten minutes after the official starting time. Community is important. One of the issues in many small group/class environments is the lack of connectivity among the people. People walk around inspired and resourced, but they remain disconnected from other believers. Foster an environment where community is developed but, at the same time, is not distracting. Distraction tends to be a problem that plagues small group settings more than classes.

Welcome: Greet everyone as they walk in. If it is a small group environment, as the host or leader, be intentional about connecting with each person as they enter the meeting space. If it is a church class environment, it is still recommended that the leader connect with each participant. However, there will be less pressure for the participants to feel connected immediately in a traditional class setting versus a more intimate small group environment.

Refreshments and materials: In the small group, you can serve refreshments and facilitate fellowship between group members. In a class setting, talk with the attendees and ensure that they purchase their *Shifting Atmospheres* study guide and book. Ideally, the small group members will have received their study guide and book prior to Week 1, but if not, ensure that enough copies of the study guide and books are present at the meeting for each person to pick up or purchase.

Call the meeting to order: This involves gathering everyone together in the appropriate place and clearly announcing that the meeting is getting ready to start.

Pray! Open every session in prayer, specifically addressing the topic that you will be covering in the upcoming meeting time. Invite the presence of the Holy Spirit to come, move among the group members, minister to them individually, reveal Jesus, and stir greater hunger in each participant to experience *more* of God's power in their lives.

Introductions

(10 minutes—first class only)

While a time of formal introduction should only be done on the first week of the class/session, it is recommended that in subsequent meetings group members state their names when addressing a question, making a prayer request, giving a comment, etc., just to ensure everyone is familiar with names. You are also welcome to do a short icebreaker activity at this time.

Introduce yourself and allow each participant to briefly introduce him/herself. This should work fine for both small group and class environments. In a small group, you can go around the room and have each person introduce himself/herself one at a time. In a classroom setting, establish some type of flow and then have each person give a quick introduction (name, interesting factoid, etc.).

Discuss the schedule for the meetings. Provide participants an overview of what the next eight weeks will look like. If you plan to do any type of social activities, you might want to advertise this right up front, noting that while the curriculum runs for eight weeks, there will be a ninth session dedicated to fellowship and some type of fun activity.

Distribute study guides and books to each participant. Briefly orient the participants to the study guide, explaining the 10–15 minute time commitment for every day (Monday through Friday). Encourage each person to engage fully in this journey—they will get out of it only as much as they invest. The purpose for the daily reinforcement activities is *not* to add busywork to their lives. This is actually a way to cultivate a habit of Bible study and daily time renewing their minds, starting with just 10–15 minutes a day. Morning, evening, afternoon— *when* does not matter. The key is making the decision to engage.

Worship

(15 minutes—optional for the first meeting)

Fifteen minutes is a solid time for a worship segment. That said, it all depends upon the culture of your group. If everyone is okay with doing 30 minutes of praise and worship, by all means, go for it!

For this particular curriculum, a worship segment is highly recommended, as true and lasting transformation happens as we continually encounter God's presence. And as you will learn in the study, it is a way to shift the atmosphere.

If a group chooses to do a worship segment, usually they decide to begin on the second week. It often takes an introductory meeting for everyone to become acquainted with one another, and comfortable with their surroundings before they open up together in worship.

On the other hand, if the group members are already comfortable with one another and they are ready to launch immediately into a time of worship, they should definitely begin on the first meeting.

While it has been unusual for Sunday school/church classes to have a time of worship during their sessions, it is actually a powerful way to prepare participants to receive the truth being shared in the *Shifting Atmospheres* sessions. In addition, pre-service worship (if the class is being held prior to a Sunday morning worship experience) actually stirs hunger in the participants for greater encounters with God's presence, both corporately and congregationally.

If the class is held mid-week (or on a day where there is *no* church service going on), a praise and worship component is a wonderful way to refresh believers in God's presence as they are given the privilege of coming together, mid-week, and corporately experiencing His presence.

Prayer/Ministry/Testimony Time

(5–15 minutes)

At this point, you will transition from either welcome or worship into a time of prayer, ministry, and/or sharing testimonies of what has happened since the last time the group met.

Just like praise and worship, it is recommended that this initial time of prayer be five to ten minutes in length; but if the group is made up of people who do not mind praying longer, it should not be discouraged. The key is stewarding everyone's time well while maintaining focus on the most important things at hand.

Prayer should be navigated carefully, as there will always be people who use it as an opportunity to speak longer than necessary, vent about the circumstances in their lives, or potentially gossip about other people.

At the same time, there are real people carrying deep needs to the group and they need supernatural ministry. The prayer component is a time where group members will not just receive prayer, but also learn how to exercise Jesus's authority in their own lives and witness breakthrough in their circumstances.

This prayer time doubles as a ministry time, where believers are encouraged to flow in the gifts of the Holy Spirit. After the door is opened through worship, the atmosphere is typically charged with God's presence. It is quite common for people to receive words of knowledge, words of wisdom, prophetic words, and for other manifestations of the Holy Spirit to take place in these times (see 1 Cor. 12). This is a safe environment for people to "practice" these gifts, take risks, etc. However, if there are individuals who demonstrate consistent disorder, are unceasingly distracting, have problems/issues that move beyond the scope of this particular curriculum (and appear to need specialized counseling), or have issues that veer more into the theological realm, it is best for you to refer these individuals to an appropriate leader in the church who can address these particular issues privately.

If you are such a leader, you can either point them to a different person, or you can encourage them to save their questions/comments and you will address them outside of the group context, as you do not want to distract from what God is doing in these vital moments together.

Some weeks you may wish to just share testimonies instead of opening it up for prayer/ministry time. God is going to be doing a lot in everyone's lives, and as they test out what they learn during the week, they are going to want to share what happened with someone. Ask if anyone wants to share stories of risks they took the week before to shift the atmosphere. This can be a way for you to celebrate each other's victories and inspire each other to take risks and try out what you hear Dawna speak about to shift the atmosphere in your daily lives.

Some people may want to ask questions about what they discerned and how they could have handled it better, so this will be a learning opportunity and a chance for you and possibly other group members to give feedback as well.

Transition Time

At this point, you will transition from prayer/ministry/testimony time to watching the *Shifting Atmospheres* DVDs.

Group leaders/class teachers: It is recommended that you have the DVD in the player and are all ready to press "play" on the appropriate session.

Video/Teaching
(20–25 minutes)

During this time, group members will fill in the blanks in their participant workbooks. Some but not all of the information they need to complete this assignment will appear on screen during the session. There will be additional information that appears on screen that will *not* go in the "fill in the blank" section. This is simply for the viewer's own notation.

Scripture

We have selected a Scripture passage that accompanies the theme for the week. You or someone else can read this out loud.

Summary

There is also short summary of the week's topic before the discussion questions. You can read this prior to the group meeting to provide you with a summary of that week's session.

Discussion Questions
(20–30 minutes)

In the Leader's Guide there will be a number of questions to ask the group, most of which are in the workbook also. Some questions will be phrased so you can ask them directly, others may have instructions or suggestions for how you can guide the discussion. The sentences in bold are directions for you.

Some lessons will have more questions than others. Also, there might be some instances where you choose to cut out certain questions for the sake of time. This is entirely up to you, and in a circumstance where the Holy Spirit is moving and appears to be highlighting some questions more than others, flow in sync with the Holy Spirit. He will not steer you wrong!

As you ask the question in the group setting, encourage more than one person to provide an answer. Usually, you will have some people who are way off in their responses, but you will also have those who provide *part* of the correct answer.

The problem with many curriculum studies is in the question/answer section. Participants may feel like the conversation was lively, the dialogue insightful, and that the meeting was an overall success; but when all is said and done, the question, *"What do I do next?"* is not sufficiently answered.

This is why every discussion time will be followed with an activation segment.

Activation
(5–10 minutes)

- Each activation segment should be five to ten minutes at the minimum, as this is the place where believers begin putting action to what they just learned.
- The activation segment will be tailored for the session covered.
- Even though every group member might not be able to participate in the activation exercise during the group time, it gives them a visual for what it looks like to demonstrate the concept that they just studied and they could try it on their own later.

Goal

After the activation exercise, we have included a brief summary of the "Goal" from that unique session. This is what participants should walk away from each session knowing and applying.

Plans for the Next Week
(2 minutes)

Remind group members about daily exercises in the study guide. Encourage everyone to participate fully in this journey in order to get the most out of it. The daily exercises should not take more than 15–20 minutes and they will make an ideal 40-day themed Bible study.

Be sure to let group members know if the meeting location will change or differ from week to week, or if there are any other relevant announcements to your group/class. Weekly e-mails, Facebook updates, and text messages are great tools to communicate with your group. If your church has a database tool that allows for communication between small group/class leaders and members, that is an effective avenue for interaction as well.

Close in Prayer

This is a good opportunity to ask for a volunteer to conclude the meeting with prayer.

SESSION 1

Understanding the Spirit Realm

Prayer Focus: Ask the Lord to help every participant understand the visible and invisible realm, their authority in Christ, and the importance of getting free from lies they are believing and unforgiveness. Pray for a greater connection to the Father, Holy Spirit, and Jesus also.

Fellowship, Welcome, and Introductions

(20-30 minutes—for the first meeting)

Welcome everyone as they walk in. If it is a small group environment, as the host or leader, be intentional about connecting with each person as they come to the meeting space. If it is a church class environment, it is still recommended that the leader connects with each participant. However, there will be less pressure for the participants to feel connected immediately in a traditional class setting versus a more intimate small group environment.

In the small group, serve refreshments and facilitate fellowship between group members. In a class setting, talk with the attendees and ensure that they receive their *Shifting Atmospheres* study guide and book.

Introduce yourself and allow participants to briefly introduce themselves as well. This should work fine for both small group and class environments. In a small group, you can go around the room and have each person introduce him or herself, one at a time. In a classroom setting, establish some type of flow and then have each person give a quick introduction (name, interesting factoid, etc.).

Discuss the schedule for the meetings. Provide participants an overview of what the next eight weeks will look like. If you plan to do any type of social activities, you might want to advertise this at the start, noting that while the curriculum runs for eight weeks, there will be a ninth meeting dedicated to fellowship and some type of fun activity. However, you might come up with this idea later on in the actual study.

Distribute study guides and books to each participant. Briefly orient the participants to the study guide, explaining the 15–20 minute time commitment for each day. Encourage each person to engage fully in this journey—they will get out of it only as much as they invest. The purpose for the daily reinforcement activities is *not* to add busywork to their lives. This is actually a way to cultivate a habit of Bible study and daily time pursuing God's presence, starting with just 15–20 minutes. Morning, evening, afternoon—*when* does not matter. The key is making the decision to engage.

Opening Prayer

Worship

(15 minutes—optional for first meeting)

If a group chooses to do a worship segment, often they decide to begin on the second week. It usually takes an introductory meeting for everyone to become acquainted with one another and comfortable with their surroundings before they open up in worship.

On the other hand, if the group members are already comfortable with one another and they are ready to launch right into a time of worship, they should definitely go for it!

Prayer/Ministry/Testimony Time

(5–15 minutes)

There won't be any testimonies since this is the first week of the study, but feel free to open it up for prayer requests and ministry if you have time.

Video/Teaching

(20 minutes)

Scripture

For by him all things were created, in heaven and on earth, visible and invisible, whether thrones or dominions or rulers or authorities—all things were created through him and for him (Colossians 1:16).

Summary

There is more to this world than what meets the eye. There are invisible forces influencing us on a daily basis. As believers, we have the ability as sons and daughters of the Most High God seated in heavenly places, to shift the atmosphere around us. Our connection to Father God, Jesus, and Holy Spirit is vital to shifting atmospheres.

In this session, Dawna De Silva addresses the spiritual realm and offers some techniques on how to stay free from the corresponding atmosphere's influence. She helps us differentiate between atmospheres we are experiencing (those we normally face) and broadcasts we are "picking up" from either other people or the spiritual realm around us. Once we identify the atmospheres that are not our own, we can shift them and exchange their influence for the Lord's blessings (love, joy, peace, etc.).

Discussion Questions

(25–30 minutes)

1. This session was about how there is a visible realm and an invisible realm that influences us. If you have been aware that this is true, raise your hand. If this is a new concept for you, raise your hand. (**This is to help you gauge where your group is at.**)

2. Have you ever gotten in a disagreement with someone and realized it partway through or afterwards that there was a spiritual force enticing you to argue? If you have a story to share, please do.

3. (**If you have a younger group, these next questions will be appropriate. If not, skip them or just ask the first and last questions.**) Have you noticed a trend in media and books toward storylines with vampires, werewolves, zombies, and other creatures? Are there any movies, shows, or books that you have seen or read that mimic spiritual realities? Feel free to share. Why do you think these types of stories are so popular?

4. Dawna shared the story about God speaking to her, "We live out our days until the Lord takes His Beloved home" through the book of Job right before she found out her stepmother passed away. Have you ever heard a timely word from God as you were reading Scripture? Could you share a story with the group?

5. In addition to reading the Word of God and allowing God to speak to us through it, Dawna talks about the importance of communicating with Jesus, Father God, and Holy Spirit. If you have realized that people have stronger relationships with either Father God,

Jesus, or Holy Spirit and feel closer to certain parts of the Godhead than others, raise your hand. If you have never really thought about it before, raise your hand.

6. Did any of you have an epiphany when she shared the story about the biker at the end?

7. How many of you are familiar with Sozo ministry? Raise your hands if you are. Part of Sozo ministry is to identify lies we believe and to close any open doors we have to fear, sexual sin, the occult, and hatred or bitterness. Dawna says, "Find out what it is inside that hooks you so that when Satan comes and talks to you, he can find no fault in you." How important do you think identifying lies, closing open doors, and making sure we don't have hooks inside of us is to successful spiritual warfare? Why?

Goal: The goal of this exercise is to start the process of identifying hooks we may have and get rid of them with the Holy Spirit's help. This exercise can be repeated as many times as is needed.

Activation: Identifying and Healing Hooks

Toward the end of the video Dawna led us in a prayer to identify hooks, which are any lies we are believing or open doors we have to sin, and give them to God. We want to go through that prayer one more time and give the Holy Spirit room to bring things to the surface so we can take care of them.

When we pray and ask God questions, we're expecting God to answer us right away. It may be in the form of an internal voice or it may be in the form of a mental picture. Remember that God wants to speak to us more than we want to hear His voice. Let's say these prayers out loud together. (**If everyone has a study guide, the group can read the italicized prayers out loud together as you prompt them. Otherwise, you can read the prayers and have the group repeat them out loud after you.**)

Ask, *"Holy Spirit, are there any hooks in me?"* (**Pause for five seconds.**)

Ask, *"Holy Spirit, what is this hook?"* (**Pause for three seconds.**)

Ask, *"Where did this hook come from?"* (**Pause for ten seconds.**)

Ask, *"Holy Spirit, who do I need to forgive?"* (**Pause for ten seconds.**)

This next part you can either pray silently or quietly. Pray this prayer: *"I choose to forgive [person's name] for what they [did or didn't do] and for making me feel [insert emotions]. I release them from all judgment."* Feel free to add your own words and pray that back to the Lord. (**Pause for a minute.**)

Now say, *"Holy Spirit, I choose to give this [insert the name of the hook/lie/open door] back to You, knowing that You are all-powerful and You won't give it back. What will You give me in exchange?"* Write down what He is giving to you in exchange. This might be a picture or it might be a promise or a Scripture. (**Pause for two to three minutes.**)

> *Say, "Thank You Holy Spirit for leading me into freedom and revealing truth to me. I receive what You have given to me in exchange for what I gave You. Please fill me up with more of You."*

Invite a couple of people to share what God showed them.

Plans for the Next Week

(2 minutes)

Point out Day 1 through Day 5 in the workbook. Encourage everyone to participate fully in this daily journey in order to get the most out of it.

Close in Prayer

WEEK 1

Video Listening Guide

We need to shift what the enemy is saying.

A third of the angels fell.

When we forget there is an invisible realm, we start fighting against the visible realm.

Satan is not at war with God. He is at war with God's children.

In the Sozo world, the open doors are: fear, sexual sin, the occult, and hatred.

Unless a Christian believes a lie, he/she will not sin.

We need to stop pausing at the door of Jesus and boldly walk through both to Father God and to Holy Spirit.

Our normal should look like Jesus.

SESSION 2

TACTICS OF THE ENEMY

Prayer Focus: Pray that each participant hears God's voice clearly for themselves so that they can become aware of tactics and lies the enemy has been using to hook them and so they can be free as they forgive and receive God's truth.

FELLOWSHIP AND WELCOME

(15–20 MINUTES)

Welcome everyone as they walk in. Be sure to identify any new members who were not at the previous session, have them introduce themselves so everyone is acquainted, and be sure that they receive the study guide and book.

In the small group, **serve refreshments and facilitate fellowship** between group members. In a class setting, talk with the attendees—ask how their week has been and maintain a focus on what God *has done* and *is doing*.

Encourage everyone to gather in the meeting place. If it is a classroom setting, make an announcement that it is time to sit down and begin the session. If it is a small group, ensure everyone makes their way to the designated meeting space.

OPENING PRAYER/WORSHIP

(15–20 MINUTES)

When it comes to the worship element, it can be executed in both small group and church class settings. While a worship time is not mandatory, it is highly encouraged, as the fundamental goal of this curriculum is to foster each participant's increased understanding and outworking of the supernatural realm. This is where true, lasting transformation takes place. Worship is a wonderful way of opening each session and setting everyone's perspective on what the class is about—not accumulating more information, but pursuing the One who is at the center of it all.

Prayer/Ministry/Testimony Time

(5–15 minutes)

Video/Teaching

(20 minutes)

Scripture

According to the working of his great might that he worked in Christ when he raised him from the dead and seated him at his right hand in the heavenly places, far above all rule and authority and power and dominion, and above every name that is named, not only in this age but also in the one to come (Ephesians 1:19-21).

God, being rich in mercy, because of the great love with which he loved us, even when we were dead in our trespasses, made us alive together with Christ—by grace you have been saved— and raised us up with him and seated us with him in the heavenly places in Christ Jesus (Ephesians 2:4-6).

For we do not wrestle against flesh and blood, but against the rulers, against the authorities, against the cosmic powers over this present darkness, against the spiritual forces of evil in the heavenly places (Ephesians 6:12).

Summary

The enemy has certain tactics that he uses to distract us and get us into battles we were not meant to fight. The good news is that once we are aware of these tactics, we will be less apt to fall prey to their strategies and more equipped to stand strong. One of the enemy's tactics is deception—getting us to believe lies about the demonic realm, ourselves, others, and God. Satan is, after all, the father of lies (see John 8:44).

In this session we will learn about common tactics and lies of the enemy, and how we can overcome them with the truth. Jesus said He is *"the way, and the truth, and the life"* (John 14:6) and the Holy Spirit loves to reveal truth to us. There are some powerful tools in this session for recognizing lies and replacing them with God's view of the situation. Don't be alarmed if some lies come to the surface. Be glad thatGod is bringing them into the light so that we can receive wholeness!

Discussion Questions
(25–30 minutes)

1. Dawna says that both extremes of focusing too much on the demonic realm and not acknowledging it at all are dangerous. Why is that?

2. What should we be doing instead of focusing on the demonic? (**Answer from the video: We should be asking the Holy Spirit, "Holy Spirit, what do you want me to know?"**)

3. Sometimes, we might start to feel sorry for ourselves when the enemy is attacking us, and then start to blame God for the attack or for not protecting us, which is exactly what the enemy would like us to do. Have you ever done that?

4. What are some solutions to win the battle over fear? (**Answers from the video: Find Jesus in the room, tell fear to go, remember your position with Christ seated in the heavenly realm, don't let fear or nightmares be bigger than they are.**)

5. According to Ephesians 6 we are in a war, but what do we learn in Ephesians 1 and 2 that should comfort us? (**Answers from the video: Ephesians 1:20-21 says that Jesus is seated above the demonic realm and Ephesians 2:4-6 says that Christ raised us up and seated us in heavenly places when we accepted Him as our Lord and Savior.**)

6. What are some common lies we believe about the enemy? (**Answers from the video: The demonic is bigger and more powerful than God or the demonic isn't real.**)

7. What are some common lies we believe about ourselves that disempower us? (**Answers from the video: I'm worthless, I'm too frail, I'm powerless against the enemy.**)

8. What are some common lies we believe about others? (**Answers from the video: They are just mean, they don't care about me.**)

9. What are some common lies we believe about God? (**Answers from the video: God isn't concerned about me, He doesn't care about what I think or feel, He doesn't protect me.**)

Goal: We want to expose any lies we are believing about ourselves, others, or God and replace those with the truth so that the enemy does not have a place to hook us.

Activation

Identifying Lies and Replacing Them With Truth

We want to take some more time to let the Lord bring any lies we are believing to the surface. Let's say these prayers out loud together. (**If everyone has a study guide, the group can read the italicized prayers out loud together as you prompt them. Otherwise, you can read the prayers and have the group repeat them out loud after you.)**

Ask, *"Holy Spirit, is there a lie that I am believing about me?"* (**Pause for three seconds.**)

Ask, *"What is the lie?"* (**Pause for ten seconds.**)

Ask, *"Holy Spirit, where did I learn this lie?"* (**Pause for ten seconds.**)

If it was from a person or institution, forgive them. You can pray this prayer out loud quietly or silently. *"I choose to forgive [insert person or institution's name] for teaching me the lie that [insert lie]. I forgive them for [what they did or didn't do] and making me feel [insert how you felt]. As I forsake this lie I release [person or institution's name] and myself from judgment."* (**Pause for twenty-five seconds or so to give people time to forgive.**)

Ask, *"Holy Spirit, what's the truth?"* (**Pause for twenty seconds and then read the section below.**)

Write down what you see or hear when you asked Holy Spirit for the truth. Only write down the good. You don't have to keep a record of the bad memories, lies you believed, or forgiveness prayer you prayed. (**Pause for thirty seconds to a minute to let people write before moving on.**)

Now ask, *"Holy Spirit, are there any lies I am believing about someone else? What are they?"* **(Pause for ten seconds.)**

Ask, *"Holy Spirit, what is the truth?"* **(Pause for twenty seconds.)**

Write down the truth. **(Pause for thirty seconds to a minute to let people write before moving on.)**

Ask, *"Holy Spirit, how would you like me to choose to partner with the truth for this person?"*

Write down what the Holy Spirit tells you. **(Pause for thirty seconds to a minute to let people write before moving on.)**

As Dawna said in the session, sometimes we think we are fighting people, but actually we're fighting against the wounds inside of them. Once we recognize what wounds they have, we can decide not to partner with those, and we can choose to partner with the truth.

Now ask, *"Father God, are there any lies I am believing about you? What are they?"* (**Pause for ten seconds.**)

Ask, *"Father God, where did I learn this lie?"* (**Pause for fifteen seconds.**)

If He shows you a person or institution, pray through this forgiveness prayer out loud quietly or silently. *"I choose to forgive [insert person or institution's name] for teaching me the lie that [insert lie]. I forgive them for [what they did or didn't do] and for misrepresenting Your nature. As I forsake this lie I release [person or institution's name] and myself from judgment. I break agreement with this lie. You, Father God, are not like a lot of people, and I let this go."* (**Pause for twenty-five seconds or so to give people time to forgive.**)

Ask, *"Father God, what is the truth?"* (**Pause for twenty seconds.**)

Write down the truth that you hear or see. (**Pause for thirty seconds to a minute to let people write before moving on.**)

Plans for the Next Week
(2 minutes)

Encourage group members to stay up to date with their daily exercises in the *Shifting Atmospheres* study guide.

Close in Prayer

WEEK 2

Video Listening Guide

If the enemy can distract us, then we're fighting a battle that's not the right battle.

We must remember that we are seated with Christ and the very things that are attacking us are coming from an invisible realm that we have authority over.

Fear is one of the biggest tools that the enemy uses against us.

The enemy wants us to believe we are powerless against him.

The enemy wants us to believe lies about: ourselves, others, and God.

Self-sufficiency takes you out of the heavens with Christ and puts you down in the level of fighting man.

The enemy wants your worship rather than you worshiping God.

SESSION 3

Weapons of Our Warfare

Prayer Focus: Pray that God shows each participant what effective spiritual weapons are and how to use them. Pray that He would also show them if they have been engaging in battles with people around them rather than spiritual warfare.

Fellowship and Welcome
(10–15 minutes)

Welcome everyone as they walk in. Be sure to identify any new members who were not at the previous session, and be sure that they receive the study guide and book.

Encourage everyone to congregate in the meeting place. If it is a classroom setting, make an announcement that it is time to sit down and begin the session. If it is a small group, ensure everyone makes their way to the designated meeting space.

Opening Prayer/Worship
(15–20 minutes)

Prayer/Ministry/Testimony Time
(5–15 minutes)

Video/Teaching

(20 minutes)

Scripture

For the weapons of our warfare are not of the flesh but have divine power to destroy strongholds. We destroy arguments and every lofty opinion raised against the knowledge of God, and take every thought captive to obey Christ (2 Corinthians 10:4-5).

Summary

In the last session we learned about tactics of the enemy. Recognizing the schemes of the devil is crucial to victorious spiritual warfare. In this session, we'll be learning about what it looks like to use *"divine power to destroy strongholds"* (2 Cor. 10:4). Dawna explains five weapons of spiritual warfare that we can use to thwart the attacks of the enemy including: the Word of God, worship, prayer, the fruit of the Spirit, and obedience. There are many ways to use each one, so get ready to be even more equipped for the battle!

Discussion Questions

(25–30 minutes)

1. This session was all about spiritual weapons of warfare. Why do you think we don't always view things from a spiritual perspective when we encounter resistance? What are some common responses you have that are not spiritual?

2. The first weapon of warfare is the Word of God, in other words, the Bible. What are some ways we can use the Word of God against the enemy?

3. The second weapon of warfare is worship. Dawna shared a story about her singing a worship song when a demon was harassing her friend and it left. What are some ideas on how you can use the weapon of worship to defeat the enemy or stories you have about worship shifting the atmosphere?

4. Dawna says, "Worship displaces the demonic, confuses them. Why? Because they are under a fallen worship leader. And when real worship happens they're confounded." Who can explain this reasoning? (**Answer: Satan was originally a head worship angel in**

Heaven called Lucifer. He rebelled and wanted to be worshiped, so God cast him out of Heaven and one third of the angels chose to go with him. Lucifer became Satan and the other angels that went with him became demons.)

5. The third weapon of warfare is prayer. Does anyone want to share a story about how a situation was changed due to divine intervention after someone prayed?

6. The fourth weapon of warfare is embracing the fruit of the Holy Spirit: love, joy, peace, patience, kindness, goodness, faithfulness, gentleness, and self-control (Gal. 5:22-23). Dawna shared a story of her son Cory laughing in a Sozo session when a demon started to talk through a lady, and then the demon and the woman's headache left. Do you have any stories or examples of how we can use the fruit of the Spirit to defeat the enemy?

7. The fifth weapon of warfare is obedience. Obedience can be submitting to someone in authority over you and doing what they say, or it could be obeying what you know the Word of God says in the midst of temptation. Do you have a story of when you obeyed (either a person or God) or when someone under your authority obeyed and it turned out well?

Goal: The goal of this activation is to uncover anything holding us back from wielding the weapon of obedience. After we forgive and repent, we can pick it back up again and use it in a healthy way with healthy people. We also want to start intentionally using weapons that God prompts us to use.

Activation

Freeing Ourselves to Use the Weapon of Obedience

We're going to go through the prayer that Dawna led us through at the end of this session more slowly to identify if anything is preventing us from using the weapon of obedience. (**If everyone has a study guide, the group can read the italicized prayers out loud together as you prompt them. Otherwise, you can read the prayers and have the group repeat them out loud after you.)**

Ask, *"Jesus, have I given up the weapon of obedience because of harm? If so, why?"* (**Pause for ten seconds.)**

If He shows you some people to forgive, pray this: (**If everyone has a study guide you can read this out loud together as a group, but if not, then you as the leader can read it out loud and pause halfway through each sentence to allow the group time to repeat the prayer after you.)**

"Father God, I choose to forgive people in my life who have harmed me through control, manipulation, and fear. I have put down my weapon of obedience because I misunderstood its power and I didn't want to use it with unhealthy people. Holy Spirit, will You train me how to start practicing with this weapon with whom it is safe to obey so that I can take it back to powerfully tear down strongholds? In Jesus's name, amen."

Ask, *"Holy Spirit, what other weapon of warfare do you want me to practice wielding this week? What will that look like?"* (**Pause for ten seconds.**)

Write down what He says to you. (**Give them a minute to write.**)

Partner up with one other person and share what weapon God said He would like you to practice wielding this week. Be intentional to ask your partner the following week if you used the weapon and how it went. (**Give people two or three minutes to partner up and share.**)

Plans for the Next Week

(2 minutes)

Encourage group members to stay up to date with their daily exercises in the *Shifting Atmospheres* study guide.

Close in Prayer

WEEK 3

Video Listening Guide

Weapons of our warfare are not of the flesh.

They are:

- The Word of God
- Worship
- Prayer
- Embracing the fruit of the Holy Spirit: love, joy, peace, patience, kindness, goodness, faithfulness, gentleness, and self-control.
- Obedience

The three seats of motivation in man's heart are: fear, love, and selfish ambition.

It is important that we pray from the right seat, the seat of love.

SESSION 4

Spiritual Authority

Prayer Focus: Pray that the Lord would unveil places where disappointment and lies have taken root, causing unbelief in God, and that the Lord would encounter each participant in powerful ways with His truth and love.

Fellowship and Welcome

(10–15 minutes)

Welcome everyone as they walk in.

Encourage everyone to congregate in the meeting place. If it is a classroom setting, make an announcement that it is time to sit down and begin the session. If it is a small group, ensure everyone makes their way to the designated meeting space.

Opening Prayer/Worship

(15–20 minutes)

Prayer/Ministry/Testimony Time

(5–15 minutes)

Video/Teaching

(20 minutes)

Scripture

Jesus came to them and said, "All authority in heaven and on earth has been given to me" (Matthew 28:18 NIV).

I have given you authority to trample on snakes and scorpions and to overcome all the power of the enemy; nothing will harm you (Luke 10:19 NIV).

Summary

Jesus has given us authority over the enemy our relationship with Him. Yet sometimes it doesn't feel that way. When things don't turn out the way we think they should, doubt can creep in about God's goodness and the truth of who we are in Him and what Jesus paid for on the cross. At the end of this session we're going to allow God to uncover any places that we've unknowingly partnered with unbelief so that He can heal those places.

As we learn about different weapons of spiritual warfare, it is vital that we stay in constant communication with God to know which weapons and strategies to use in each situation we face. Just because we have a lot of weapons or tools in our tool belt, doesn't mean we should use them all at once. God knows which ones will be effective in specific situations. He loves to communicate with us and He wants us to be victorious in every battle!

Discussion Questions

(25–30 minutes)

1. Why do you think Jesus told His disciples, *"I have given you authority to tread on serpents and scorpions, and over all the power of the enemy, and nothing shall hurt you. Nevertheless, do not rejoice in this, that the spirits are subject to you, but rejoice that your names are written in heaven"* (Luke 10:19-20)?

2. Dawna says we should pay attention to the hierarchy of the demonic, not to be afraid of how big they are, but for what reason? (**Answer from the video: The strategies to displace them might be different.**)

3. Mark 6:5-6 says Jesus *"could do no miracle there except that He laid His hands on a few sick people and healed them. And He wondered at their unbelief"* (NASB). Some people believe that faith has a tremendous part in miracles taking place and others say that neither our amount of faith nor the recipients' lack of faith should affect the miracle. What role do you believe faith has in miracles happening?

4. After lies are removed and demonic agreements are released, what are keys to the person staying free? (**Answer from the video: Replace the vacant space with truth and relationship with Father God, Jesus, and the Holy Spirit.**)

5. Why isn't it a good idea to automatically command spirits to bow or to leave places when you sense they are there? (**Answer from the video: We need to check with God to see what He wants us to do. The people in that place may be partnering with the spirits and not want them to leave. You might experience some retaliation from the enemy if you do something outside of what you have permission from God to do.**)

6. When you recognize you are facing something larger than you have faith for, what do you do or what do you think you should do? (**Some answers might be: Listen to or read testimonies of that problem bowing to Jesus, ask a faith-filled friend to pray on your behalf, remind yourself of God's promises in the Bible, hang out with people who have authority in that area, sing a faith-filled song, and go through Dawna's prayer below.**)

Goal: To get rid of unbelief and increase our faith in God so the enemy has no place to hook us. To let God show us what attribute of Him in us is our strongest weapon.

ACTIVATION

Dislodge Unbelief and Identify Your Strongest Weapon

This activation is meant to help us identify and dislodge lies that are causing unbelief in our lives. We'll be going through a similar prayer to what Dawna led us through at the end of the video more slowly and let the Holy Spirit bring truth into places where we have unbelief. (**If everyone has a study guide, the group can read the italicized prayers out loud together as you prompt them. Otherwise, you can read the prayers and have the group repeat them out loud after you.**)

Ask, *"Holy Spirit, is there unbelief in me?"* (**Pause for three seconds.**)

Ask, *"Are there situations in my life that I have felt you won't come through?"* (**Pause for fifteen seconds.**)

Ask, *"What lie am I believing about these situations?"* (**Pause for fifteen seconds.**)

Ask, *"Jesus, what is the truth that you want me to know?"* (**Pause for fifteen seconds.**)

Write down what He says to you. (**Give them a minute to write.**)

Pray this prayer: (**If everyone has a study guide you can read this out loud together as a group, but if not, then you as the leader can read it out loud and pause halfway through each sentence to allow the group time to repeat the prayer after you.**)

> *"I hand to You, Jesus, any unbelief in this situation and I ask You to exchange it for the truth that You are all powerful, and that my weapons are divinely powerful for tearing down strongholds. Unbelief go! Faith, come! Holy Spirit take the place where unbelief resided so there is no waterless place inside of me for the enemy to attach. In Jesus's name, amen."*

For the next section of our activation, ask, *"Jesus, what attribute of you in me is my strongest weapon? Why is that?"*

Write down what He says to you. (**Give them thirty seconds to write.**)

Plans for the Next Week
(2 minutes)

Encourage group members to stay up to date with their daily exercises in the *Shifting Atmospheres* study guide.

Close in Prayer

WEEK 4

Video Listening Guide

If Jesus has been given all authority to overcome, He's given you also the authority.

Do you know Him? Does He know you?

Sometimes it's helpful to get support and get others to pray.

Unbelief can be blocking our authority.

Unforgiveness and bitterness hold people in their own prisons.

Who has the key to that jail cell? Two answers: you and God.

We need to move when God says move, and we need to stand and sit when God says stand and sit.

SESSION 5

Discerning Spiritual Atmospheres

Prayer Focus: Pray for each participant to be able to discern spiritual atmospheres so that they can shift them when needed. Pray for revelation on ways they already have been picking things up and impartation to begin recognizing the atmospheres in new ways.

Fellowship and Welcome

(10–15 minutes)

Welcome everyone as they walk in.

Encourage everyone to congregate in the meeting place. If it is a classroom setting, make an announcement that it is time to sit down and begin the session. If it is a small group, ensure everyone makes their way to the designated meeting space.

Opening Prayer/Worship

(15–20 minutes)

Prayer/Ministry/Testimony Time

(5–15 minutes)

Video/Teaching

(20 minutes)

Scripture

Solid food is for the mature, who because of practice have their senses trained to discern good and evil (Hebrews 5:14 NASB).

Summary

An important part of shifting atmospheres is discerning the prevailing atmosphere. Similar to our physical senses (taste, touch, sight, hearing, and smell), our spiritual senses allow us to pick up information. Whether the topic of discerning spiritual atmospheres is brand-new information for you or not, we can all grow in the gift of discernment.

As you listen to Dawna share stories that illustrate ways we can discern, see if you can recall times that you have sensed the spirit realm in similar ways. Expect to receive an upgrade in your discernment by listening to this teaching and discussing it with your group. As you grow in this gifting, it will be helpful to pray with other like-minded believers. Pay attention to who God might be highlighting for you to connect with in this next season.

Discussion Questions

(25–30 minutes)

1. What is a spiritual atmosphere? **(Answer from the video: A spiritual tone or mood.)** What causes a negative spiritual atmosphere? **(Answer from the video: The demonic realm releasing broadcasts and people partnering and creating a place for those broadcasts to land.)**

2. Although this session focuses on shifting negative atmospheres, what are some examples of positive heavenly atmospheres? Can you share a story?

3. Have you ever smelled the demonic or angelic? Can you share a story?

4. Have you ever sensed or felt the demonic or angelic? Can you share a story?

5. Have you ever seen (either with your physical eyes or in your mind's eye) the demonic or angelic? Can you share a story?

6. You can have three voices in your head: the enemy, yourself, and God. It can take time and practice to be able to recognize the source of what you are hearing. How can you tell which voice is talking?

7. Have you ever had a dream that gave you insight into the spiritual atmosphere? Can you share a story?

8. If we sense the demonic is attacking someone, what can we do? **(Some answers could be: Pray and ask God what the strategy is for you to help and do what He shows you to do, pray protection over them, or pray the opposite for them.)**

Goal: Practice discerning the prevailing atmosphere, getting feedback from other people, and asking the Holy Spirit what to do with what you sensed.

Activation

Discern the Atmosphere in the Room

In this activation we want to practice the gift of discernment in this very room. Dawna says that one way we can become sharper in our discernment is to ask other people what they are sensing, and if it is the same as what you are sensing, that could be confirmation. This is not always the case. More than one person can be wrong but it is one way to grow.

(This is going to be an open discussion and activation time. It could go in many different directions. Just follow the Holy Spirit and practice!)

What do you sense in the atmosphere in this room?

Ask the Holy Spirit where it came from. What did you hear?

If it wasn't a positive broadcast you sensed, ask the Holy Spirit what He wants you to do about it. As long as the group leader agrees, do what the Holy Spirit showed you to do (this could be for the group to do or just you).

Plans for the Next Week

(2 minutes)

Encourage group members to stay up to date with their daily exercises in the *Shifting Atmospheres* study guide.

Close in Prayer

WEEK 5

Video Listening Guide

A negative spiritual atmosphere is a combination of the demonic realm releasing broadcasts and us partnering and creating a place for those broadcasts to land.

Negative atmospheres in our life come from the lies we are believing and the hooks inside of us where sin still has a place.

How do we discern spiritual atmospheres?

- Smell
- Sense or feel
- See
- Hear
- Dreams

You can have three voices in your head: the enemy, yourself, and God.

Just because you pick up something going on around you that's being broadcast doesn't mean it's yours. That's why we have to know what we're free from.

When we sense the demonic around someone, it could be because they are partnering with it or it could be that they are being attacked by it.

SESSION 6

Shifting of Atmospheres

Prayer Focus: Pray that each participant would get a firm understanding of the steps to shift an atmosphere and be able to start practicing on a regular basis.

Fellowship and Welcome

(10–15 minutes)

Welcome everyone as they walk in.

Encourage everyone to congregate in the meeting place. If it is a classroom setting, make an announcement that it is time to sit down and begin the session. If it is a small group, ensure everyone makes their way to the designated meeting space.

Opening Prayer/Worship

(15–20 minutes)

Prayer/Ministry/Testimony Time

(5–15 minutes)

Video/Teaching

(20 minutes)

Scripture

Do not participate in the unfruitful deeds of darkness, but instead even expose them; for it is disgraceful even to speak of the things which are done by them in secret. But all things become visible when they are exposed by the light, for everything that becomes visible is light (Ephesians 5:11-13 NASB).

Summary

Now that we have learned about recognizing prevailing spiritual atmospheres, it is time to learn the next steps in order to shift the atmospheres. Of course these steps should be taken with the guidance of the Holy Spirit. Consciously deciding to not partner with whatever atmosphere you encounter and then sending it back to where it came from is the next step. After that, asking the Holy Spirit what to release in its place is the last step. Once you get a firm understanding of these steps, you can apply them to shift most atmospheres you encounter.

We will also be hearing stories of how Dawna approaches bringing up the topic of negative spiritual atmospheres with her family and friends to get their feedback and to help them get free from the demonic influences if need be. Let these stories be an encouragement for you to do the same!

Discussion Questions

(25–30 minutes)

1. The second step after we discern a negative atmosphere is renouncing it. What does that look like?

2. The third step after we renounce a negative atmosphere is asking God what to release in its place. What does that look like?

3. When the enemy's broadcasts feel truer than the higher spiritual reality, what should we do?

4. If you ask someone else if they are sensing what you are sensing and they say "no," what are the possibilities? (**Answers from the video: They could be right and that spirit is not in the atmosphere, they could not be picking up on it, or you just may not have identified where it is coming from and it is not in you.**) What should we do then? (**Answer**

from the video: Ask the Lord for more insight into what you sensed and see what He shows you.)

5. Dawna shares about how she asked her boys if they were struggling with temptations when she had dreams or sensed san abnormal broadcast or atmosphere. Oftentimes they were struggling and then they were able to have a conversation about it. Is this something you could see yourself doing with your family, people you live with, or close community?

6. Why does it feel risky to bring things into the light by sharing what you are sensing and asking others to give you feedback?

7. What are the benefits of bringing your discovery into the light?

Goal: To become more comfortable with the steps to shifting atmospheres.

Activation

Practicing the Steps to Shifting Atmospheres

Think of a negative atmosphere you encountered earlier today or are encountering right now. We are going to go through the steps to shift that atmosphere together out loud. (**Give the group ten seconds to think of an atmosphere. Then tell them that if they could not think of one, they should still participate. If everyone has a study guide, you can read through these steps together. If they do not, you can read through each step and pause after each one to let the group repeat after you.**)

Say, *"I see you [insert negative spiritual atmosphere]. I am not partnering with you. I send you back."*

Ask, *"Holy Spirit, what do you want me to release in its place?"* (**Wait twenty seconds and then encourage the group to pray and release silently what the Holy Spirit told them to release.**)

If you noticed an immediate shift and feel comfortable sharing, share what you sensed with the group. (**Ask group members to share.**)

Plans for the Next Week

(2 minutes)

Encourage group members to stay up to date with their daily exercises in the Shifting Atmospheres study guide.

Close in Prayer

WEEK 6

Video Listening Guide

The second step after discernment is renunciation.

The third step is displacement.

Most of the time shifting atmospheres looks like discerning it, renouncing it, and displacing it.

It is important that you learn what your normal state of being is so that you know that what moves you from your normal is not you.

Ask God to show you what is real.

Bringing things into the light helps people realize it is not a war they are fighting on their own.

SESSION 7

Shifting Atmospheres Over Yourself and Your Home

Prayer Focus: Pray that each participant would be brave enough to let God's light illuminate their atmospheres and have the courage to do what needs to be done to shift those atmospheres if needed.

Fellowship and Welcome

(10–15 minutes)

Welcome everyone as they walk in.

Encourage everyone to congregate in the meeting place. If it is a classroom setting, make an announcement that it is time to sit down and begin the session. If it is a small group, ensure everyone makes their way to the designated meeting space.

Opening Prayer/Worship

(15–20 minutes)

Prayer/Ministry/Testimony Time

(5–15 minutes)

Video/Teaching

(20 minutes)

Scripture

Finally, brethren, whatever is true, whatever is honorable, whatever is right, whatever is pure, whatever is lovely, whatever is of good repute, if there is any excellence and if anything worthy of praise, dwell on these things (Philippians 4:8 NASB).

Summary

In this session Dawna addresses the need for us to become aware of the atmospheres we give off personally and the atmospheres we steward in our homes. As children of God, we should be promoting heavenly atmospheres. Dawna gives us simple tools to identify what is causing the negative atmospheres to develop so we can deal with them and invite God's presence to fill the void.

As we implement these tools, not only will we experience more joy and peace, but the world around us will be influenced by God's presence emanating out of us. Who knows what transformation will take place as a result?

Discussion Questions

(25–30 minutes)

1. Why is it important to know what atmospheres we are giving off?

2. What should we do when we become aware that we are giving off a negative atmosphere? **(Answer from the video: Find out what the root of it is and then take care of it. If you've been sinning, repent. If you're believing lies, renounce them and start believing the truth. If you need to forgive, forgive.)**

3. Have you ever noticed that what you dwell on, you broadcast? Can you share a story?

4. Have you ever been inside of a house or building and noticed a positive atmosphere? Can you share a story?

5. What atmosphere do you want in your home? **(Go around the room and have everyone in the group share one or two things.)**

6. What have you found to be effective to shift a negative atmosphere in your home? You don't have to disclose who or what was necessarily causing the negative atmosphere, but can just say what was an effective solution.

7. If you have already noticed your home giving off godly atmospheres and affecting people in positive ways, share why you think this is happening so that the group can get ideas for how they can do this in their home also.

Goal: To identify what atmospheres we are giving off and get rid of the root of any negative atmospheres so that we can start stewarding heavenly atmospheres.

Activation

Identifying and Shifting Atmospheres Over Ourselves and Our Homes

In this activation we will be going through similar prayers to what Dawna led us through in the video and allowing God to speak to us about atmospheres we give off and give us keys to shifting those atmospheres if needed.

(If everyone has a study guide, you can read through these steps together. If they do not, you can read through each step and pause after each one to let the group repeat after you.)

Ask, "*Holy Spirit, is there an ungodly atmosphere I give off?*" **(Pause for three seconds.)**

Ask, "*Why do I give this off?*" **(Pause for ten seconds.)**

Ask, "*What do I need to do to make this right?*" You might need to forgive someone, renounce a lie, or repent for sin. Go ahead and do that now. **(Pause for a minute and give them time to do business with God.)**

Ask, "*Father God, what atmosphere am I supposed to be giving off?*" **(Pause for ten seconds.)**

Ask, "*What do I need to know to partner with this atmosphere?*"

Write down what He says to you. **(Give them a minute to write.)**

Ask, *"Holy Spirit,* what atmosphere do you want in my home*?"* **(Pause for ten seconds.)**

Ask, *"Holy Spirit, is there a lie I am believing about my household or someone living in my house?"* **(Pause for ten seconds.)**

Ask, *"What is the truth?"*

Write down what He says to you. **(Give them thirty seconds to write.)**

Ask, *"Holy Spirit, is there something ungodly that we have been doing in our home that I need to repent of?"* Go ahead and do that now. **(Pause for thirty seconds.)**

Ask, *"Holy Spirit, is there someone in my house that I need to forgive? Do I need to forgive myself?"* Go ahead and do that now. **(Pause for thirty seconds.)**

Ask, *"Holy Spirit, what atmosphere do you want in my home?"* **(Pause for ten seconds.)**

Ask, *"What do I need to know to partner with this atmosphere?"*

Write down what He says to you. **(Give them a minute to write.)**

Plans for the Next Week
(2 minutes)

Encourage group members to stay up to date with their daily exercises in the *Shifting Atmospheres* study guide.

Close in Prayer

Video Listening Guide

It is important to know what atmosphere we are giving off.

Negative atmospheres we give off come from lies we believe and sin.

When you dwell on an atmosphere, it starts broadcasting back out of you.

How do people respond to you? If it is negative, one of two things are happening: You're either giving off an atmosphere that they are responding to or they are listening to a target against you. If it is the second one, ask God to dismantle their hearing ears to the voice of the enemy.

We should, as a family, be cheerleaders for each other.

SESSION 8

Shifting Atmospheres Over Regions

Prayer Focus: Pray that each participant would get a firm understanding of how to displace regional spirits and not succumb to their influence.

Fellowship and Welcome

(10–15 minutes)

Welcome everyone as they walk in.

Encourage everyone to congregate in the meeting place. If it is a classroom setting, make an announcement that it is time to sit down and begin the session. If it is a small group, ensure everyone makes their way to the designated meeting space.

Opening Prayer/Worship

(15–20 minutes)

Prayer/Ministry/Testimony Time

(5–15 minutes)

Video/Teaching

(20 minutes)

Scripture

If My people who are called by My name will humble themselves, and pray and seek My face, and turn from their wicked ways, then I will hear from heaven, and will forgive their sin and heal their land (2 Chronicles 7:14 NKJV).

Summary

We've reached the final session of *Shifting Atmospheres*. In this session we will learn how to recognize and displace regional spirits. There are hierarchies to the angelic and demonic realm and certain angels and demons can have authority over regions. When we pick up broadcasts from a regional spirit, there are certain steps we can take to release a heavenly broadcast. Dawna shares several examples of what this looks like. As always, we should stay connected to the Holy Spirit and ask Him for strategies in how He wants us to release the goodness of God.

Be encouraged, mighty warrior! You have been thoroughly equipped for the battle and are positioned to win!

Discussion Questions

(25–30 minutes)

1. Why do certain demonic forces have a right to be in certain places? **(Answer from the video: People are sinning by partnering with the demonic broadcasts.)**

2. Dawna shares how she was led to call upon the name of Jehovah Sabaoth, the Lord of Hosts, when she needed heavenly reinforcements. Have you ever called upon one of God's names like this? If you do this on a regular basis, how have you become familiar with the different names of God?

3. Oftentimes we don't realize what regional spirits are over the place where we are from. Is there a spiritual atmosphere you've recognized in your home city? When and how did it become apparent to you?

4. Have you ever traveled somewhere and recognized a regional spirit? How did that come about?

5. What are the steps to displacing a regional spirit? **(Answer from the video: Repent for any ways you've partnered with it, repent on behalf of people in the region that have partnered with it, ask God what He wants you to release in its place, and do what He shows you to do.)**

6. Have you ever done a prophetic act over a region or a piece of property? What did that look like? Did you notice a change in the atmosphere?

7. How do you feel about displacing regional spirits? Do you feel like it is doable?

Goal: To recognize a regional spirit in your area and as a group get the strategy from God to release the opposite and do that.

Activation

Release the Opposite Spirit in Your Region

In this activation you will target a specific regional spirit in your area in the way God shows you. (**This could go in a number of directions, but you get to lead it. You may wish to pray beforehand about if there is a specific regional spirit God wants you to target, and present that to the group. Otherwise, spend some time in prayer with your group and see what God shows you to target.**)

Agree as a group which specific regional spirit you will target.

Keeping in mind the elements to displace a spirit (humble yourself, repent for ways you may have partnered with that spirit/sin, forgive anyone who partnered with the spirit/sin in that area, and release what God shows you in the way He shows you), pray out loud together as a group.

Ask God what strategy He wants you to take to release the opposite spirit into the region. Discuss that with the group and if possible, do it today. If it will require more time than you have, consider setting up a time to do it on a different day as a group.

Plans for the Next Week

(2 minutes)

Let participants know that either this is the final week of the study or that you will be having some type of social activity on the following week—or at a specified future date.

Close in Prayer

Pray that the group would truly be able to shift atmospheres with the Lord as they continue to daily walk out the tools that have been presented throughout the course.

Video Listening Guide

There is an order in the angelic and demonic realm.

One way to tell if you are dealing with a regional spirit is if you cannot change the channel easily.

The best way to stay under authority for regional issues: humble yourself, repent, and forgive anyone who partnered with the sin in that area.

One strategy to displace a regional spirit is by doing the opposite.

We shift the atmosphere by not partnering with it and releasing a military move of the opposite.

Looking for more from Dawna DeSilva and Bethel Church?

Atmospheres 101 by Dawna De Silva

https://shop.bethel.com/products/atmospheres-101

Boundaries by Henry Cloud, John Townsend

http://www.boundariesbooks.com/boundaries-books/boundaries/

Brave Communication by Dann Farrelly

https://shop.bethel.com/products/brave-communication

Recipe for a Fear-Free Life by Dawna De Silva

https://shop.bethel.com/products/recipe-for-a-fear-free-life

Shirtless in My Offering by Stephen De Silva

https://shop.bethel.com/products/shirtless-in-my-offering

Someday When I'm Young by Cory De Silva

https://shop.bethel.com/products/someday-when-i-m-young

SOZO Saved Healed Delivered by Dawna De Silva and Teresa Liebscher

https://shop.bethel.com/products/sozo-saved-healed-delivered-a-journey-into-freedom-with-the-father-son-and-holy-spirit

Stepping Through the Door of Jesus by Dawna De Silva

https://shop.bethel.com/products/stepping-through-the-door-of-jesus

The Three Battlegrounds by Francis Frangipane

https://www.amazon.com/Three-Battlegrounds-Depth-Spiritual-Heavenly/dp/1886296383/ref=tmm_pap_swatch_0?_encoding=UTF8&qid=1497189728&sr=8-

Who do You Think You Are? by Ray Leight

https://shop.bethel.com/products/who-do-you-think-you-are-volume-1

Wielding the Weapon of Obedience by Dawna De Silva

https://shop.bethel.com/products/wielding-the-weapon-of-obedience

LEADER'S NOTES

www.ingramcontent.com/pod-product-compliance
Ingram Content Group UK Ltd.
Pitfield, Milton Keynes, MK11 3LW, UK
UKHW060612180726
13836UKWH00012B/2516

9 780768 415704